The Korean Soul

The Korean Soul

A Collection of Poems

H. C. Kim

The Hermit Kingdom Press
Seoul   Bangalore   Cebu City

Cheltenham (USA)

The Korean Soul:

A Collection of Poems

© 2002 by H. C. Kim

The Hermit Kingdom Press
Seoul, Korea
Bangalore, India
Cebu City, Philippines

ISBN: 0-9723864-0-8

The Hermit Kingdom Press
Cheltenham, Pennsylvania, USA
http://www.TheHermitKingdomPress.com

info@TheHermitKingdomPress.com

*I would like to dedicate these poems to the memory of
Raoul Wallenberg*

Preface

I have always wanted to publish a collection of poems about the Korean experience, but have not been able to do so until now. I wish that I had started earlier because it was a deeply rewarding personal experience for me. I promise that these poems are only the beginning. I feel that there are many great things about Korea that others around the world could share, and I would love to play a part in the process of enlightenment. I hope that you will enjoy these poems.

H. C. Kim
Jesus College
Cambridge
U. K.

Acknowledgements

I would like to thank Tim Kao of Westminster Theological Seminary, Dr. Clifford Bates of the University of Warsaw, and Miso Park of Newnham College, Cambridge, for their willingness to read some of the poems and comment on them.

I would also like to thank Pyeong-Eok An of Darwin College, Cambridge, the current President (2001-2002) of the Cambridge University Korean Society, for his interest in the poems.

I would further like to thank Professor Gabriel Jonsson, the Professor of Korean Studies at Stockholm University, for his kindness and for offering comments on the whole manuscript.

Lastly, I would like to thank my best friend Ed Moseng for his constant encouragement.

Table of Contents

"Toilet Paper"

Every history has its quirky side
A tale that spreads through the countryside
One such story is one about how
Christianity entered the countryside
It's a true one to be sure
Because there are personal testimonies to the effect

In the earliest times
When American Christian missionaries
Did not know Korean very well
They started their missions work
By passing out Bibles translated in Korean
To all who were interested in reading it

They would memorize few key phrases to be sure
"This shows the way to Heaven!"
They would shout in Korean
Sometimes, they shouted just the word
"Heaven"
Some people took the Bible because paper was precious

Often American Christian missionaries
Proclaimed the Gospel in the countryside
Poor areas
Where paper was precious
Paper was welcome
Although the missionaries might not have been so much at first

How were these Bibles used?
Often, they were placed near the toilet
And used as toilet paper
After the business was done
One cut a few pages out of the Bible to use it as wiping paper
How horrendous, you say?

Well, often the Bible accomplished more than
Merely being used as toilet paper
Some doing their "thing"
Got bored and read pages from the Bible in Korean
And there, right in the midst of it all
Some accepted Jesus Christ as their personal Savior God

For God so loved the world
That He sent His only begotten Son
That whosoever believes in Him
Shall not perish
But have everlasting life
That moved the heart of the Korean unbeliever

There is no place where God is not
And this applies to the bathroom
So, it is not surprising that some found Christianity there
There is no regulation in Christianity against accepting Christ there
In early days of the history of Christianity in Korea
This was the case

Some of the converted
Toilet paper converts
One might call them
Became Christian ministers who shared their testimony
Others became lay leaders
You can't knock the power of this toilette paper

"Tick"

What makes a Korean tick?
No doubt this question has been asked many times before
By friend and foe alike
What is the impetus of the Korean spirit?

Generosity
They say this is a mark of the Koreans
Koreans love to give and give
It's ingrained in the culture

Is it the spirit of generosity that motivates a Korean?
The desire to do good
Under normal circumstances
Show exceeding kindness

If so
How great it would be to be the recipient of this motivating spirit
To be able to partake of the kind spirit
To participate in the good

But to every ying
Is its corresponding yang
Look at the Korean flag
It is characterized by the ying-yang principle

If Koreans love to give and give
Good and kind things
Then they are also capable of dishing out
The corresponding opposite

Treat a Korean with genuine kindness
Generosity and kindness will flow in your direction
Abuse a Korean
Then there could be endless retribution

What makes a Korean tick?
For a friend as well as a foe
It might be better to ask
How can I become deserving of his ying and not his yang?

———— ⚮ ————

"Through the Marketplace"

Hold mom's hand tight, okay?
Mom goaded the boy
Too small to be spotted
In a busy marketplace
With a worried look in her eyes

There were stories of how
Small boys got lost in the market place
And could not find their parents for hours
That must be frightening to a small boy
In a crowed place with unfamiliar faces

The Korean open air market was big
It sure did to the little boy
Who could hardly see much above
The big giants' knees
Naturally, he held his hand high and held onto mommy dearest

There was a vendor selling only underwear
White ones
Colored ones
Those with Korean characters written on them
It attracted a lot of customers

Over there
The boy could see
Toys
He tugged at his mom's hand
Trying to lead mom there

Mom
Mom
Can we go see the
Toys?
The boy goaded

No time for
Toys
Dear son
We had better get what we need
And we have to meet up with daddy

Oh
Mom
I want to see the
Toys!
Toys!

Okay
We'll stop by for a second
Mom
Usually of strong resolution
Was weak before her son whom she loved

A toy was added to the pile
To the smile of the boy
Who held mom's hand tighter
Holding the toy with the other
On their way they went

Through the marketplace
As the flood of people rushed at them
Noises all around
Conversation as well as yelling
The boy was happy

Mom bought what she needed
Each time
She haggled
And reduced the price
Which was obviously intentionally inflated

Mom smiled
Because she thought that she had a great deal
The sellers were happy because they knew they made a profit
The boy was happy because he had his toy and his mom
Through the market place they went, mom and son, together

"Three Musketeers"

One
Two
Three
We are three musketeers!

How funny it must have looked
As three boys gathered
To offer eternal allegiance to each other
In friendship

We will stand by each other
Through the hard times and the bad
Because we are
Three musketeers

How easy the oath seemed back then
To make
With not much life lived
Not knowing exactly what lay ahead

Now
I wonder
If it was foolishness back then
Or if cynicism has captured me now

Could I make the same kind of allegiance today?
Promising to give up my life freely and willingly
For the other musketeers
Why not?

I wonder if others remember
The solemn oath that we made
In the way only those under 10 years old could
To protect each other at all cost

We all believed in our promises
In the honor of friendship
And idealistic fidelity
We thought we would be three musketeers forever

Those days in Korea stand out in my mind
As we played our silly three musketeer games
Jumping off high places
Running about the small neighborhood in Seoul

I wonder how many people that I see in the street
Had their three musketeer teams
Way back when
I hope that they did have that experience

———— ❦ ————

"The Walk"

The walk seems long and endless
For miles and miles
Only the dirt road stretches forth
Will the road ever come to an end?
It is a country road

The view is not so unpleasant
To either side of the road
There are fields
Grassy areas
And farmlands too

But the road is consistently brown
Dirt road
Not much to look at
Almost harsh
Austere

What lies beyond?
Nothing
It seems
But I know that there is something at the end of it
There is the ancestral mountain

On that mountain
Are buried ancestors
Spanning generations
It is my connection to the past
To the land

It lets me know
What my lineage is
It is my belonging
A part of my identity
Self

It is a long walk
To the sacred mountain
A kind of identity marker
But even this holy mountain was profaned
By the foot of colonialism

———⚬———

"The Train Ride"

Speedily the train rushed from point A to point B
Point A being Seoul
Point B being Pusan
From the biggest city in Korea
To the second biggest

From the city of the boy's current residence
To the city of his birth
From the city of his education
To the city of pre-education days
As if traveling back in time

The train rushed
As if the past were much better than the present
The trees quickly seemed to fly in the other direction
Houses, too
Inside the train, people sat looking out their stationary window

Sitting next to dad
In the first long train ride of his life
The little boy felt brave at first
After all, it was just men traveling this time
But the bravado did not hold too long

Only a few minutes inside the fast moving vehicle
Realizing soon enough that the whole ride will be without mom
In his own way understanding that it wasn't just a visit to the
    grandparents'
But a stay without mom
Who is to give birth to his sister to be

The boy
Only a few years after the zygote state
Cried tears
And they were not man's tears either
Crying shamelessly for "mom"

The train did not stop at the boy's cry
Shouting order
It consistently moved along
Towards the final destination
Away from the city where mom was waiting

She was waiting for the dad to drop off the son
Whom she loved
She knew that he would be happy with his grandparents
In time, after a while
That did not stop her worrying with a mom's heart

The train rushed
As boy cried
He did not know what went through his mom's heart
Or his dad's either
All he knew was that he wanted to be home

In time the boy's tears dried up
He could shed no more tears
His voice was hoarse and he could not shout as loudly
It wasn't that he was giving up
Physically, it was no longer possible

The train was steadfast
It ran and ran
With a noise that made its presence known
As some of the passengers fell asleep
The boy fell asleep, too

Sleeping there on the train
In his fetal position
The boy was carried towards the place of his conception
To be embraced by the parents of his dad
Their son

Like the magic carpet
The train traveled smoothly through the air
Although bound to the ground by gravity
It sped toward its destination
As if to change the times

"The New Year"

The New Year is an important holiday in Korea
It's not just a day to recover from New Year's Eve parties
Or merely to vegetate in front of the TV
It's an active holiday
With much movement

Children are decked out in traditional Korean outfits
Clothes that provide a connection to the hundreds of years of history
At least
They walk around the neighborhood
Pay their respects to the neighborhood elders

After they have paid their respects to older family members
With each sign of respect
They receive a little cash
A western equivalent?
Halloween and trick-or-treat

In Korea
The New Year custom plays a social role
Reminding the members in the society of the social cohesion that exists
The way the community is ordered
One might even call it a social ritual

In its communal focus
Korean New Year's Day
Might resemble the American Thanksgiving
When family members come from miles and miles away
Although turkey is not often consumed in Korea on these occasions

There is ample food to be sure
All kinds of meats
Regional specialties find their accentuation on the tables
Who can forget the delicate rice cakes?
They just melt in your mouth

And they are not made of chocolate
There are distinctive foods consumed rarely during the year
So children await eagerly for the New Year
There is more than special food
Special games are played

Family members gathered around
To play the traditional Korean game
"Yoot"
Is its name
Every Korean boy has played it at least once

The Korean New Year
Is a family bonding holiday
A social phenomena
A subconscious reaffirmation of identity
Special to all

———— ❦ ————

"The Hat"

As a boy I remember
Looking at the hat
Worn by old gentlemen
With long white beards
And completely white clothing

These traditionally clad
Korean gentlemen looked
So dignified
Their white hair appeared
I bet not only in the pictures

These hats
Transparent but black
Kind of like black top hat
With circular base
But you could see their heads inside the Korean hats

Funny how a hat could add dignity
A presence to an individual
But many bearers of the hat
Seem like they earned the respect
Many surely had a full and fulfilled life

I wonder how I would look in a hat like that
With the white Korean outfit
With white hair
And long white beard
I guess I would have to travel back in time to wear such an outfit

"The Cry of the Enslaved"

Koreans cried out in their servitude
With no visible prospect for freedom in sight
As the oppressors laughed
And did impose their will

So is the cry of the oppressed
It probably sounded like the cry of the Palestinians
As the Jewish State stamp their feet
On the dignity of the Palestinian people

Koreans cried out in their oppression
Having difficulty seeing God who is just
In the midst of all the suffering
But they persevered and Christians continued to believe in Christ

So is the lot of the oppressed
It must be similar with the Palestinians
Many of whom continue to believe in God's blessing
As the Jewish state starves its people

Koreans cried out in their righteous anger
They had done nothing wrong
But they were painted as people deserving of such treatment
Power's voice is always heard

So is the case with the downtrodden
How many Palestinian journalists have you seen on CNN?
Such a contrast to the number of Jewish journalists on TV
Postmodernism teaches that all these Jewish journalists have an agenda

Koreans cried out in helplessness
As powerful nations sought their political interest
Selfishly they made an implicit pact
To allow all of it to happen

So is the experience of the little people
Palestinians are the underdogs
They are painted by powerful states
At best, as invisible

"The Bullet"

How cruel was the bullet
That struck down the young boy
In his prime
He was just minding his own business
A good boy he was

But the stray bullet
Did not discriminate
It did not know that the boy was good
Nor did it care
It struck and took his life

Such is war
They say
And it did happen during the Korean War
What horrible battle it was
A nation in turmoil

But what does the bullet care
It just flies and accomplishes its mission
It hits and kills
And doesn't care who the opponent is
Like a good lawyer, it represents the interests of its client

It was so
That one fateful day
When a young Korean lad
Walked on that path
To his dying breath

His mom had lost her husband
In the Korean War
Because the invading Communists
Were offended by his Christian faith
And killed the young preacher before he saw his first daughter marry

Only a short time, thereafter
The still mourning widow
Saw her only son die
By a stray bullet
That wasn't meant for her son

The owner of the gun was an American soldier
Who came to protect her and her family
Yes, even her son
From the invading Communists
But it was his bullet that took the life of her beloved

The son was young with bright hopes
People say that he was intelligent like his mom
Had leadership skills like his dad
That he would do a lot of good for the Korean people
And for the whole world as well

It was not the bullet of his enemy that killed him
The murdering bullet belonged to an American soldier
Who alleged fidelity to him and all on his side
The American soldier shot his gun in anger
Because the newspaper boy ripped him off

It was equivalent to a few bucks
Perhaps less
But the soldier missed his home
And his family
He resented the war

He took out his frustrations
With the gun that he was holding
Forgetting that it was an instrument of death
It had become a part of him
So he shot and expressed his anger that way

The bullet flew
Obeying its master
But the master's command was not so precise
It flew past the newspaper boy
And struck down an innocent boy roughly his age

Did the dutiful son die for the newspaper boy?
If one can say, "Yes"
Perhaps the death was not in vain
But one can't even say that
For, the bullet had missed the newspaper boy before its kill

The son died instantaneously
The mother was without a son
Who followed the path of his father
The mom must surely still remember
As she prays for the American soldiers and their safety

—————— ⧖ ——————

"The American Missionary"

Every nation has its history
And some remember the quirky
Distinctive elements
That stand out

Such is the American missionary
You can't say that he is so foreign to Korean history
Because he colored the pages of it
Like the way he colored the Korean countryside with his whiteness

With candy in hand
The American missionary gathered Sunday School children
Some of whom became major leaders in the Korean church
Others became political leaders

He came in self-abnegation
He purposely chose the poor areas
And lived among them
Perhaps imitating the vagrant life of Christ

And his work bore fruit
The message spread like wildfire
The biggest Presbyterian church in the world is in Korea
So is the biggest Baptist church and the biggest charismatic church

How the American missionary suffered
He suffered together with the Korean people
He went through the Japanese occupation
Was jailed with Korean Christians

The American missionary stood by Koreans
During the Korean War
And shared the Gospel message of love
And audacity

There are not enough books
Written about the American missionary
And the good he did in Korean history
For a testimony

"Taekwondo"

Do you remember how all those Korean black belts
Young and old
Lined up to break wood
In the opening ceremonies of the Olymics
Held in Korea a while back?

Wasn't that the coolest thing that you have ever seen?
Perhaps, it's because I appreciate the sport
Martial Arts, they call it, sometimes
That I thought the choreographed sequence
Awesome

I remember that an elementary school in the neighborhood
Required all its students to take Taekwondo classes
For gymn
You would not want to mess with those kids
They will surely put their learning to productive use

I took Taekwondo classes
There were a half dozen Taekwondo masters at my dad's church
Although I did not start learning it until I immigrated to the USA
This made it that much more special
It was like discovering roots

I did feel connected to the past
After all, my Korean ancestors produced this art form
Who says that martial art isn't art?
In the same way western dance is, it is
Like ballet, there is beauty to the form

I will never be able to jump and do a simultaneous kick
With both my legs
In the air
Like my dad's black belt master friend
But I could appreciate how difficult it is

Some Taekwondo masters
Skipped high school to fine-tune their art form
They were often apprenticed under established masters
Those Martial Arts movies were not kidding at all
Taekwondo is an important part of the experience

Yes, it is true
We did not have anything like the Boxer's rebellion
Taekwondo was never really seen as an offensive art
Rather it was learned for self-defense
And for the art form

So why not experience this aspect of Korean culture?
Put on that white Taekwondo suit
Do some stretches
And learn to kick and block
Like those Korean masters of old

"Student Demonstrators"

Freedom!
We shall be free indeed
Did the student demonstrators shout in their hearts
As they protested colonialism
That has assailed the Land of the Morning Calm
And created a permanent storm and discord
For thirty-five years

Why should we be subjugated in the land where
We and our ancestors have lived for hundreds of years?
This is our land!
They can't just come in
With their advanced military weapons
And subjugate us!
So the voices of Korean students rose

With guns they disdain the language that has been spoken here for years
They are even requiring us to learn their imported language
That has not been spoken in this land
Certainly not for thousands of years
Creating a situation in which using our own language becomes worthless
With violence they force us to use their language for daily living
The righteous indignation of Korean students found its meaning

With their whole future in front of them
Student demonstrators took to the streets
Not caring whether they would be jailed
Or even shot
They stood up for freedom
Against the oppression of the colonizers
Indeed, some demonstrators were jailed and others killed

Students demonstrated
Not in a foolhardy manner
But in logical assessment
Freedom was a virtue
Besides, colonialism did not afford them a future
In their own land
Where their ancestors have lived for hundreds of years

These Korean student demonstrators
Were willing to stand up and protest
Because there was no future without such a public objection
Their lives would be empty and without meaning
When the oppressing armies caused them to fear each day
No hope to live as Koreans with dignity and human worth
Some things were worth fighting for – dying for

Korean students marched
With determination
Not knowing what their seemingly weak protest
Would bring about
But being certain that engaging in civil disobedience
Was better than taking injustice lying down
Pen-held hands in the library were replaced by enclosed fists in the
streets

They walked
Ran
Stepped side to side
But did not crawl
They were there to show that they were human beings
With dignity and rights
In the land that they inherited from generation to generation

No colonizer was going to steal their land away
And dictate terms for living
Without a registered protest
These Korean student demonstrators were there to make sure of that
Even if they did not see freedom in their life time
They found meaning in active civil disobedience against an oppressive
   regime
Colonizers get out!

———— ⚭ ————

"Spirit Unbroken"

What is it about the Korean spirit that spurs perseverance?
During the Japanese occupation
Colonialism failed to break the Korean spirit
Despite all the humiliation
And persecution

During the Korean War
People learned what death is
The most horrific kind
Poverty and dearth of everything
But Koreans continued

Koreans represent spirit unbroken
It's even evident in the Koreans who are abroad
Koreans in the USA
Koreans in Russia
Koreans in China

They were all sojourners
Visitors in the land
Foreigners
Immigrants
But they have kept their spirit

Koreans will continue to progress
And go forward
Because they have spirit unbroken
In the midst of the greatest difficulty
Even when they had nothing, they had the Korean spirit

What is it about the collective experience of the Koreans
That produces such a spirit?
Is there something in their history?
In their culture?
Or is it that there is something special in their water?

"My War"

My war
What is my war?
How do you think the colonized answer this question?
It is against oppression

My war
A lot of questions must go into it
If colonialism is your daily experience
How will oppression end?

My war
It is not just an abstraction
A thinking process
It's an existential question

My war
The colonized do not have the liberty
For mere intellectual discussion
Their answers determine their future

My war
What is my war?
How do you think the colonizers answer this question?
It is to maintain oppression

My war
The colonizers have the latest technological weaponry
At their disposal
Often, they perceive the war as already won

My war
How should the observers answer this question?
Should we side with the oppressors or with the oppressed?
What is the right thing to do?

My war
What is my war?
Each and everyone must ask this question?
Will I do the right thing?

———— ⚮ ————

"*Morning Exercises*"

In the morning
We all gathered in the schoolyard
I remember it well
As corny music played
And the gym teacher stood in front in his jumper outfit

We lined up as straight as we could
As if we were in the army
We were only 8 years old
But we did what we were told
Like good soldiers

It was a part of the national health program
All children everywhere in Korea were doing
Similar exercises
Healthy children make
A strong nation

I don't know
How much healthier I became
But I suppose it was better than doing no exercise
More is always better
Isn't it?

I wonder if they still do the morning exercises
With loudspeakers blaring lively tunes
A middle-aged teacher in front moving his body about
Trying to strengthen the future of Korea
A healthy mind makes a healthy body

The morning exercises were fun
Looking back
It certainly left an impression in my mind
I wouldn't be surprised if other Koreans
Remember with fondness those morning exercises

———— ◯◯ ————

"*Lost*"

Lost in the streets of Seoul
A big city
No place for a small boy to get lost
What did I think about
As I walked all over?

I was told how much mom and dad worried
How they gathered all their friends to look for me
They combed all the streets
Where I had wandered away
Like a little Viking in search of adventure

All I could remember
Even now
Is all the fun I had
Wandering the streets
Looking at the sights

How mom and dad must have worried
Looking near this building
That corner
For their boy
Who they thought was afraid and alone

But no
He had brought a friend from the neighborhood
Slightly younger than he
On his big adventure
They wandered the streets together

They say ignorance is bliss
Perhaps, this is true
Not knowing all the dangers out there
The two young adventurers must have traveled
Fearlessly

There was so much to see
And do
Even at the young age
The young voyagers knew a lot was out there
Much more than the naked eye could see

The worried parents must have added
Wrinkles to their faces
Worrying
Praying
Wondering

The two partners in the journey
Weren't worried
They were merely wandering
With an open mind
To see

I don't think I was in any danger
I am not saying that there aren't any dangers out there
But I felt safe then
And obviously
A whole day's wandering was done in safety

Even at such early age
I knew to avoid the cars in heavy traffic
To walk boldly albeit with caution
After all mom and dad taught me well
They should have been more confident in what they had taught me

I know
They worried
Because they loved me
They knew all the bad things that were out there
It's in the news every day

But there are a lot of good out there too
Kind strangers lending a helping hand
People who are willing to donate their time and money
To help those in need
Seoul's streets are full of them

I remember the genuine joy
Tears of happiness
That marked the faces of mom and dad
When they "found me"
But I was never lost

H.C. Kim

"Korean Dance"

Korean dance
Troup dressed in
Traditional Korean dance outfit
Colorful like a peacock in its glory
Not just splendid clothing

But
Even a special hat as well
With a long strand of cloth
That spins round and round
With the movement of dancers' heads

The whole space
Is filled with the jumping
Koreans dancers
And their spinning headgear
With colorful impressionism of the movement

I can hear the drums
The traditional ones
Which my ancestors beheld
In rhythmic glory
With connection to the past

How beautiful it is to hear
The glory of Korea's past embodied in rhythm
To see the expression of Korea's joy and powerful emotions
In dance
To see the art and aesthetics of it all

The room is filled with awe
Some have never seen such a dance before
Others have seen it
But still marvel at the wonders of the traditional dance
Distinctively Korean

———— ⬥ ————

"Knee Deep"

I could see my relatives
Knee deep in the field
They are farmers
You see
They have the perfect tan to prove it

They have been out so long
For so many years
Their skin is permanently brown
Darker than some of my African American friends
In Philly

They have smiles plastered on their faces
What are they so happy about?
They are out in the scorching heat
In the unbearable summer humidity
With no shade to block the penetrating sunrays

They are working the land
Maybe it's the nobility in farming
That Emperor Augustus described
Farmers are the foundation of the Roman society
So went the saying

Perhaps
Korean farmers
My relatives
Feel that they are working the land
And so they own it

Perhaps
Their happiness derives from that
It could be that
They remember the Japanese occupation
When they felt that they did not own their own land

Such is the sadness of colonialism
Even the place where you live
Does not belong to you
But now
This farmland is theirs and in the real sense of ownership

With smiles
Knee deep in the field
The farmers
My relatives
Are joyfully working the land

Their smile is contagious
True contentment
Confident in who they are
That they belong to the land
They are who they are

―――――― ❧ ――――――

"Kimchee Sandwich"

Sandwich
An invention of the West
Can be modified for the Korean palate
How?

Place a slice of Wonderbread
On it put some 100% Korean kimchee
Then cover it with another slice of bread
Now you have a kimchee sandwich

How did I discover this concoction?
On a day not particularly memorable
Having run out of rice
With just kimchee jar

Well stocked
I must add
For it is a fuel of the Korean spirit
Kimchee energy, you might call it

There was no rice
The Store was far away
It was probably closed at that hour
I just had a kimchee crave

Hunger fueled by kimchee longing
Spurred creativity
I had consumed kimchee by itself before
But its satisfaction was always wanting

Kimchee with rice
Plain white rice
Is something
Really tasty particularly in moments of hunger

With longing for white rice
Korean rice that sticks and holds like glue
But lacking it
I searched the cabinets for a substitute

There before me was a smiley face so familiar on the cover of
Wonderbread packages
Why not?
I asked myself

Soon I made a sandwich
I could make a sandwich with meat
With vegetables and cheese
Why not kimchee?

Anticipation awaited the first bite
I felt the chewy layer of kimchee
And the soft texture of the bread slices
Yummy!

So was born
A new sandwich
That became my favorite
Kimchee sandwich

"Student Demonstrations"

I remember it well
One sunny
Hot
Afternoon in Pusan
Our taxi came to a standstill

Traffic was blocked
As far as eyes could see
And the smell
Of tear gas
Permeated the streets

The taxi driver shook his head
Told us that there was another student demonstration
As if it were a nuisance
What was the demonstration for?
I asked

It was for democracy
For greater rights of the people
To empower the masses
The taxi driver explained
But they had become a tradition for college students

Go to college
Then, you have to demonstrate
The driver added sarcastically
These very students when they go to the army
Will be deployed to quash the demonstrators

Useless cycle
Is it though?
Isn't there a need for demonstrations for the sake of human rights?
Expectedly, the military might try to suppress it
The antithesis to the thesis

Hegelian synthesis would result
Although students might not achieve what they want
They would have moved closer towards better conditions for the masses
So, aren't the demonstrations useful?
They are for good causes, after all

But they do block the traffic
And all in it will have forced tears
From the residue tear gas
That the summer wind carries
Is it all worth it?

Should the whole populace of Pusan be forced to make the sacrifice?
Some perceive it as the students' whims
Useless and dying tradition
What they forget is that it was because of protests like these decades ago
Real rights were granted to them, which they now enjoy

——— ⬥ ———

"Justifying Terror"

The colonialist logic
That whipping the colonized is good for them
If you don't, then they will make trouble
They are savages

Justifying terror is an art form
A prerogative of the educated
Pages after pages were written about why
Colonialism is good

Colonialism of the Korean people was good
The pro-colonialist intellectuals add
So is the opinion of such intellectuals
To the Palestinian question

What is the final solution to the Palestinian question?
To push them out into the sea and make them drown?
To oppress them and humiliate them?
To make the Jewish State feel powerful?

All would find justification through logic
Colonizers are among the most educated
It has always been that way
And it always will be

Education dulls the conscience
Brains and no balls
Some might say
The educated are often the problem of the oppressed people

When do the educated really stand up for the oppressed when it
    matters?
Look at Palestine
How many intellectuals stand up to plead their case
Brains and no balls

Koreans suffered
Korean women in the tens of thousands were shipped off as toys for
    soldiers
Western nations knew what was going on
But they kept their mouth shut

Look around you?
Which politician pleads the case of Palestinians?
Who ever speaks for the oppressed?
What always was, it always will be

Most educated people will keep their mouth tightly shut
When oppression strikes
Survival of the fittest demands siding with power
Why be destroyed with the colonized?

Choose the right team
Some might say
Often the educated do choose the "right" team
The educated justify colonialist terror

———— ∞ ————

H.C. Kim

"History Is Not"

Silence
Pervades as I ponder
The vastness of the ocean
Like the history that has gone before me
The waves come flooding in
Little by little
The sandy shore is engulfed by the deep ocean

I move my beach chair back
Again
Still wanting to bask in the Pusan sunrays
I don't want to abandon the beach
Although time has driven out the sunbathers
Flooding the beach
I can feel the coldness of the late afternoon seawater on my toes

Waters that seemed so warm before
Particularly when I was submerged in it
Soaked in the noon sunshine
Now has suddenly changed
And give me shivers down my spine
Like a sudden change in history
That shocks

Who knows what will happen in history?
It's not like in hindsight
A Korean knows what should have been done
To prevent the Japanese colonization
Looking back
It's easier to figure out
But the future?

One could have the attitude
Come what may!
Some might have had that spirit
Before the financial collapse
It certainly shocked
And shook the society in no uncertain terms
Some did hold on to their optimism

How unpredictable the currents
In world's history
What we expect today
Can be absent in tomorrow's records
GOK
God Only Knows
So Christians say

Unlike the human inability to see into the future
The incoming tide is certain
Day after day
The tide comes in
If I come back tomorrow
I will have to move the chair back
Around the same time

I gaze into the distance
I am not sure
Which continent is straight beyond the sea
I hear the birds flying in the air
I can smell the salt water
I see the tide coming in
I take a deep breath of the refreshing air

As much as I want to enjoy the warmth of the sunshine
The tide moves closer and closer towards the edge of the sand line
Temperatures are dropping
The friendly sun seems to be withdrawing its friendship
I know what's coming and grab my shirt that will give me warmth
Some things are predictable
History is not

"From the Ruins"

All was in ruins
After the Korean War
There were kids in the streets
Who had lost their parents in the war
They were fatherless

Alone
Many felt even as they gathered together as a family
They had nothing left ·
They barely survived the war
It was a horrible war

Orphans abounded
Poverty was everywhere
Those after the war were left
Picking up the pieces
Looking at a nation in ruins

Who would have imagined that a nation in ruins
Could rise up from the ruins
And be the glorious cosmopolitan nation
That it now is
No one then would have believed it

Literally
Buildings were razed to the ground
The capital of the nation looked like a junkyard
With nothing to salvage
But how appearances could deceive

Look at Korea now
It is strong
And tough enough to weather hardships like
"The IMF Crisis"
Even in its wounded state it shows how long it has come since the War

From the ruins
The visible brokenness was mended
From sadness prevailed optimism
With hope progress came
The fatherless found a future along with others destitute from the War

"For the Oppressed to Stand Up"

It was hard for Koreans to stand up against oppression
During the Colonialist period
They were socialized to respect authority
And isn't it human nature to want security?
Who wants to stand up and risk the sword of the oppressors?

Palestinians are a peaceful people
Although pro-Jewish media would want to paint them all as terrorists
Yellow journalism has a long-standing tradition, you know
They were socialized to respect authority
And they are human beings like you and me

The evil of colonialism is racism
The colonized are always inferior
Or more evil or more violent
So the Jewish State paints a picture of the Palestinians
As more violent than Jews, ethically inferior people

How else could you justify colonialism?
You can't say that you are going to come and take their money
And enslave them
You have to make it seem like you are doing the colonized a favor
Jews are in Palestine to make Palestinians less savage, didn't you hear?

There is a long-standing tradition of colonizers painting a picture
Of how the colonized need the colonizers
Just like a wife-beating husband reasons that she needs it
He is hitting her for her own good
But he still loves her, doesn't he?

The ugly face of colonialism
Whether in the past of the colonized Koreans
Or the present of the colonized Palestinians
Who are prevented from nationhood and independence
Colonizer's whip is for the good of the oppressed

Within the educational institutions of the colonizers
There is a well-reasoned, logical explanation for all of it
The colonized are illogical
They do not know what is good for them

Jews know what is best for Palestinians
If the Palestinians were given a state
Then they would self-destruct
So speak the superior race of Jews in the Jewish State

Are Palestinians innately violent people?
Are they always wanting war?
Could the Jewish media be right?
Are Jews really a superior race?

It is hard for the oppressed to stand up
Intellectuals are against them
Powerful nations are against them
It was the case in Korea and it is the case now in Palestine

———— ⬥ ————

"Final Solution"

Final solution is very important
You have to get it right
Or it will come back to haunt you

Finding the final solution is difficult
Execution of the policy is even harder
That is why there is usually no final solution

What is the final solution to end colonialism?
The colonialism in Korea ended
Because America dropped two atom bombs on Japan
Killing hundreds of thousands of people

Would you say that these deaths are bad?
Should colonialism have continued?
The Japanese civilians who died were not innocent
They had participated in colonialism

So is the case in Israel
Jews in the State of Israel are not innocent
First of all, all the males are members of the army
But even if they were civilians, without active protest, they are guilty

What is the final solution to end colonialism?
How many Jews in Israel today are even asking this question?
It is more likely they are not
They are more interested in the final solution to the Palestinian "problem"

Perhaps a final solution to end colonialism will come
The way it came in Korea
Would it be wrong if civilians died in their guilty participation in
    colonialism
If it means freedom for the oppressed?

———— ⚭ ————

"Farmer Relatives"

Most city slickers in Seoul have relatives in farm areas
In fact Seoul's population is filled with former farmers
Who sold their farms to move to the big city
In order to give better education for their kids
Who in Seoul haven't heard of farm boys in colleges in Seoul?

There are many of them
Some of them have parents who sold their farms
Their tuition is paid with parents' life savings and future livelihood
Not only do these students carry with them rural accents
That are easily detected

As a side note
Some of them become ostracized from certain circles
Because of their regional accents
Regionalism is still quite important in Korea
The upside is that regional specialties in cuisine are preserved

With the accents
These farm boys bear with them
Aspirations of their families back in the farmlands
In the boondocks of Korea's hinterlands
They are the family's hope

Some might say that Confucianism plays a strong role
The concept of parents' bond to their children
Almost a kind of heavenly obligation ingrained in the Korean psyche
Can't it be simply put, however
That it's simply parental love?

However one puts it
Sacrifice was made
A great self-giving
And in filial duty
Many of these farm boys did not disappoint

Farms were not sold in vain
As Korean economy took off
These farm boys played their part
In the Korean economy
And brought manifold returns on the sold family farm

Although successful
These farmer boys have not forgotten their roots
Watch Korean programs
And one will understand
There is a constant reminder of this social reality

Not just in documentary type programs
But in daily dramas
Soap operas
In movies
As well

In fact
Farmer relatives provide a key link to the past
When Korea was not so urban focused
When most of the country was rural
Majority of population living in farm areas

Hear ye
Farmer relatives
You are important
For the soul of the nation
And its search for identity in modernity

"*Elementary Memories*"

Those were fond memories
That I had
When I was only a lad
Aged nine

When in Seoul
I had friends
In my elementary school
And in the neighborhood as well

Playing marbles
With distinctive
Rules set by the neighborhood
Sometimes I won

Other times
I lost a whole bagful of marbles
But I wasn't mad
Because I enjoyed the game

Marbles often changed hands
From a friend
To another
Winning did not seem to matter that much

Or is it because
I am now
Grown up
Looking back?

Perhaps I did care
It is possible that I cried
A boy's tears
When I lost

And celebrated my victories
Like there was no tomorrow
As if I were the king of the neighborhood
In a way only an elementary school boy can

Such are the memories from my elementary school days
The good ones stand out
And bad ones seem distant
Even soliciting nostalgia

Do I want to bring back those days?
I don't know
Maybe
But I do know

I would not trade those elementary memories
For a million bucks
Pounds
Or Euros

I might change them
For a million won
If the pictures on the bills
Will bring me other memories from Seoul

"Duk-bok-ki"

Some say that food is a capsule of memories
When one looks at a food item
One can remember specific experiences
Feelings of joy and pain
Associated with that food

For many Koreans
One might say
Duk-bok-ki
Conjures up distinct memories
It is like cheesecake in the USA

When one is happy
One went out for a helping of Duk-bok-ki
When one felt sad
One gathered friends together
To consume Duk-bok-ki

It's not uncommon
For a guy to take a girl he likes out
To the place
That makes the best
Duk-bok-ki

You might not be wrong
If you said
Some guys' hearts were won over by women who made great
    Duk-bok-ki
And some women probably experienced the same
With great Duk-bok-ki male chef

I remember gathering up few coins together
Going to a local Duk-bok-ki place
A small hole in the wall
As a kid, I didn't care if it didn't look too sanitary
Duk-bok-ki was great and that's all that I cared about

I wonder if that small Duk-bok-ki shop is still open
I remember it being really small
And I was a small boy of nine years old
It must absolutely look tiny, now
But Duk-bok-ki was out of this world

I don't think I have ever tasted any Duk-bok-ki that matches its taste
It might be the memories that glamorize the experience
And give the taste of that Duk-bok-ki's mythic qualities
It was nice, being there with buddies
Adding to the memories

Small pieces made of flour
Dipped in spicy red pepper paste sauce
Consumed with Tempura soup on the side
There is nothing like it in the world
Particularly on a cold winter day

Duk-bok-ki just warmed you up inside
And the spicy taste lingered sweetly in your mouth
Memories to treasure the taste
For years to come
That certainly is priceless

———— ⚬⚬ ————

"*Dog Meat*"

What's the fuss anyhow?
You don't eat dog meat
Because it's not a part of the French cuisine
You might eat frog legs
Or some such exotic food

Do you see Koreans picketing in Paris
To ban frog legs
And other French foods
Prepared with dead animals?
Why do you disrupt peace in Korea?

Why is it your business that Koreans eat dog meat?
Aren't dogs animals like cows and sheep
And frogs?
It is not like you are slaughtering human beings
Like in the French Revolution

Leave Koreans to eat their dog meat
French to eat their frog legs
Eating animal meat
Is
Eating animal meat

There is nothing morally wrong in eating dog meat
Just like there is nothing morally wrong with eating meat of cows
Perhaps, if the prepared food tastes bad
Because the chef is horrible
Then he should be barred from cooking

But don't prohibit eating of dog meat
For those hot dog lovers
It is totally moral
And ethical
To eat meat of animals

"Country Boy in a Seoul University"

He spent his nights on the bench
It was a hard time in Korea
And harder for those from the countryside
City boys just could not understand

One country boy
Went begging from house to house for food
In the western tradition
There were the mendicant orders
Christian monks who were respected
No such tradition existed in Korea

But education is valued
And university students are respected
As the future promise of the nation
So the begging students were given food in generous portions
It's a country where a university ID card can be used as a guarantee
For a tankful of gasoline

How did Korea become a modern nation
From the rubbles of the Korean War
After decades of colonialism?
It was the spirit of these country boys
Who persisted and worked hard
And the nation that valued them

"Colonialism"

What can be said for colonialism?
Was it not an import from the West?
The way European Jews imported
Colonialism to Palestine

Korea suffered
A dagger was driven through the heart of a people
And twisted around and around
Such is the harm of colonialism

There was a whole generation of Koreans
Who were forbidden
Not allowed to learn Korean
Such is the cruelty of colonialism

Koreans were worked and worked
Like slaves and then humiliated
All the profits went to the colonizers
Such is the injustice of colonialism

Korean women were mistreated
Some were shipped off to be used as toys by soldiers
Colonizers feel that they own the colonized as possessions
Such is the oppression of colonialism

Korean children were prevented from a future bright
They were taught to be subservient
Inferior to the colonizers
Such is the evil of colonialism

Wealthy nations just kept their eyes closed
As colonizers were allowed to do what they wanted
Such was the colonialism in Korea and the international response
Just like the way Jews colonize Palestinians, today

"Bridges"

Why did they build so many bridges?
Do we need so many bridges as these?

You could hardly see the river
It makes the city look crowded

But the city is crowded
There are millions of people living in the city

It is Seoul after all
The soul of Korea, some say

So many Koreans living in such closed quarters
No doubt what they say is true

Koreans are experts at living in harmony
Koreans are an agreeable people

Those bridges allow
The flow of millions

Keep the society fluid
And moving

They took long time to make
A lot of sacrifices went into it

Time
Money

The bridges serve an important purpose
To bind the society as one

They are like patches on the city
That provide healing powers in a symbolic way

They are so clearly visible
So in your face

You might not say that they are so aesthetically beautiful
Although more than a few find them pleasing nonetheless

Yes, bridges are good
Those bridges are needed

A lot of effort will be exerted to keep those bridges in tiptop shape
But it will be worth the time and money, too

Those bridges will hold for our posterity
It will benefit them in concrete and certain ways

———— ⧉ ————

H.C. Kim

"An Ode to King Sejong"

Ode to you
O, King
You who formed the Korean alphabet
That we use today

It's an alphabetic system
That is quite cool
Unlike western languages
Which are linear

Each letter placed side by side
A word is formed
By several units
Placed next to each other thus

Korean is different
One syllabic unit may have a letter next to each other
But it is possible to have a letter underneath
Or above

A Korean word is formed with one or more of these units
You might call it two-dimensional
Unlike western languages
Which are one-dimensional

Horizontal and vertical units
Are visible in a Korean word
It is quite complex
And that's what I like about it

Even the alphabets are complex
And interesting
Because your mouth shapes the form
That you see on the page

For instance
Mi-um
A Korean alphabet letter
Looks like the way your mouth moves to pronounce it

So
Ode to you
King Sejong
For creating such a beautiful alphabet

I know it's not much of an ode
But I figure
The alphabet system and the language
Are ample enough ode for you

"Aid and Abet"

Why not aid and abet colonialism?
There is money to be gained
Political interest to grab
Personal profit to be made

So, some Koreans heeded the call of the colonizers
They aided and abetted the oppressors
And became fat on the blood of their countrymen
They turned a deaf ear to the oppressed

Who has not heard of Uncle Tom?
A character that provided condemnation to
African-Americans who aided the oppression of
Fellow people of color

This is the case with the Palestinians as well
As colonizers seek venue of power and control
Some will heed the call
And will aid in the oppression of Palestinians

Sometimes
The educated are the guiltiest
They have learned too well how to protect their own self-interest
Most aiders and abettors to colonialism will be found within the
    college walls

————— ⚭ —————

"Admiral Lee"

On the rough waters of the Land of the Morning Calm
He waged a fierce defensive war
Against the incoming enemies
With military genius not surpassed in the region
Winning every battle
Hard fought
With rigor
Creativity borne in the peaceful land
Desiring to defend the Morning Calm
Admiral Lee Soon Shin was his name

The attack kept coming
Relentless was the enemy
Desiring to conquer
Soldiers could easily have been demoralized
The attack was consistent
The waters were rough
Death was all around
Food was scarce
But the warriors stood fearless
With commanding Admiral Lee at the helm

The pride of the Korean navy
For centuries
Even now
The name of Admiral Lee
Emboldens the heart of the Korean soldier
His bravery
Charisma
Determination

A heart for the Land of the Morning Calm
Made him a symbol of Korea

The monument to Admiral Lee
Standing tall in Gudok Mountain
Reminds every school kid
On a trip with his mates
That there is something to be proud of in Korean history
The story of courage
The tales of triumphant defense
Sacrificial efforts
To defend the Land of the Morning Calm
What wonderful spirit of historical empathy!

One could almost hear the whisper
Firm and determined
From the dying Admiral Lee
Fatally wounded in sea battle
A command
Not to let anyone know that he has been wounded
That he will die
Prop him up and make him look as if he is alive
So that the battle will be won
His death should not discourage the soldiers

The war must be won
For the sake of the Land of the Morning Calm
To preserve what gives the Land the calm
Admiral Lee had lived and fought
All of his life
To protect and preserve the Land of the Morning Calm
And his death was not going to break the tradition of courageous
    defense
The battle will be won
And it was won
"Don't let others know of my death" was his dying words

"Kimchee"

Kimchee
Some might say that this is what makes Koreans
Koreans
Kimchee could be consumed
Breakfast, Lunch, and Dinner
And it often was
It's like a fuel
To the motorcar
Without it a Korean might not be able to function
It is a source of energy and nostalgia

How sweetly it smells
To Koreans
Who are Koreans inside and out
Kimchee smell
Keeps the juices flowing
It whets the appetite
No Korean complains of its smell
Kimchee smell permeates
In towns, villages, and cities
Where Koreans dwell

In lands where Kimchee is foreign
Where people have not even heard of its name
Have not smelled the odoriferous concoction
No doubt
Kimchee finds rejection
Kimchee smell solicits complaint
Its presence could receive the harshest ban
Perhaps there might be a polite snub

Or a fragrant display of displeasure
Even a mocking gesture or guffaw

How precious is Kimchee to Koreans
In contrast
Koreans might be found lining up
In front of a passing Korean food truck
To purchase a jar of Kimchee
Which they might not dare open until they reach the safety of their home
In lands that do not belong to Koreans
Where Koreans are only sojourners
Places were Koreans and their favorite food
Kimchee experiences rejection

There are Kimchee tales
Of how a Korean student in a Western school almost devoid of Koreans
Hid his Kimchee
And consumed it only in open air
Where the vast sky would take away the odor
Perhaps all the way back to the land where Kimchee abounds
For he heard a tale
Of how a Korean who ate Kimchee
In a university dormitory was kicked out of it
For offending Western students with an aggressive smell

Kimchee was foreign
And apparently offensive
The fear of being ostracized due to Kimchee
Caused some Koreans to abandon it for a time being
Hiding the love he has for Kimchee
His devotion hidden deeply in his heart
One needed to survive in a foreign environment
Setting foreign to Koreans
But common to those who have been there for hundreds of years
This might belong to the "Secret Tales of Kimchee"

It is certainly a part of the Korean experience in the West
There are living testimonies to these tales
In oral tradition
Stories are passed on from one Korean to another
Those who experienced it
Recounting with emotion
Others receiving the tradition with wonder and amazement
How could anyone not like Kimchee?
It's impossible!
How could Kimchee be rejected in such a manner?

Kimchee is the pride of all Koreans
It gave millions of Koreans so much joy
It continues to
And it will
It is a continuous part of the Korean history
Through the difficult periods of Korean history
Kimchee symbolized Korean solidarity
Korean identity
Even the Japanese colonizers were conquered by Kimchee
In the land of Kimchee and exported it to their land

Kimchee stands as a monument to the Korean spirit
Stark
Sharp
Strong
Always a strong presence
It spices up even the blandest of dishes
It alone with plain rice can make a tasty meal
There is nothing to match it
In the Korean mind
The Kimchee display in Korea boldly testifies to its versatility and
    staying power

"Bun-dag-yi"

Bun-dag-yi
Sold in street corners
Often placed in a cup
Made out of newspaper
Is a good stuff

If you see it
You might describe it as
Looking something like a bun
Of a queen bee
It is only a thumbnail size

Dag!
That's nasty!
You might say
When you look at it closely
For it is an insect of sorts

Be ye not
Condemn the consumers
Of
Bun-dag-yi
Though

I remember as a child
Loved eating it
It tasted good
And the juices were
Mouth-watering as well

But I do have to confess
When as an adult
I tried to consume
Bun-dag-yi
I just could not

It looked like an insect
Cooked
With juice looking like
Inner parts of insect matter
It never occurred to me so as a child

Did I change?
Bun-dag-yi
Surely didn't
I still have fond memories of consuming it
Maybe I'll try it again next time I see it

"Burnt Alive"

Human flesh burning
Smell pervading throughout the neighborhood
From which people gathered
One by one
To the morning service

Who would have thought
That they would not be able to leave the building
That this would be the end of their life
On earth
None of them probably expected it

It was one Sunday
During colonialism
In a small Korean village
Where Christians gathered
To worship the Christian God

The church
Refused to bow down
To the Shinto Shrine
As it was required by law
And Korean Christians were forced to pay the consequences

The church was boarded up
Windows shut
The fire lit
In strategic places
To maximize the burning

The building quickly caught fire
As winds were favorable for the burning
The force of the law
Under colonialism
Supported such an action

Korean Christians sang inside
Hymns that they had learnt
Some recently translated into Korean
By Christian missionaries from the West
As they slowly were engulfed in flames

Some certainly sang out of tune
Most of them were not good enough to be in a choir
But their voices were sincere
Passionate
They testified to their deep devotion

The church burned
Smoke suffocated
And the once familiar building
Was in ruins
In a brief time

Within the ashes
The rubble
Were bodies and remains
Of the saints who sang
Until the last hour

Their voices
Were testimonies of their dedication to their religion
But
Also a defiant stance
Against an unjust colonialist power

They were burnt alive
These Korean Christians
And it wasn't just at this small village
But in others as well
A chapter in Korean history

———— ∞ ————

"Children of Immigration"

Yeah
It is true
Everyone has an opinion
And
They are not afraid to let you know
Exactly what they think
You gained a few pounds
Do not fear
They will be there to point it out
So you could be "encouraged"
To go on a diet
They will probably say that directly to you
Why don't you go on a diet?
You look like you need it
The funny thing is
They say that with absolutely no malice
Sometimes
They may actually care about you
You could imagine
The Korean children of immigrants
Who grow up in the USA
Or in England
Struggling with such
Well
Shall I say
Directness
It is opposite of what they experience in schools
What they are taught as right behavior
What are these children to think?

Everyone has an opinion in the Korean society
And they are not afraid to share it
Positively
One can certainly say
That they feel comfortable enough to share their true thoughts with
    you
But the children of Koreans
In the USA or in England
Just cannot get used to it
Caught between Korean culture and the culture of the New Land

———— ⚶ ————

"Collective Memory"

There is something to be said for
Collective memory
Of all the Koreans who suffered
At the hand of colonialism
All were affected back then

The Palestinians who are suffering now
They are developing a collective memory
The young will remember
Some of them will write Ph.D. dissertations on it
It will be ingrained as they suffer

Who knows what will happen as a result of this?
History moves
Collective memory plays a part
It certainly will not be forgotten
As Palestinians suffer today

What is the value of collective memory?
I doubt that
The suffering
Have the strength to think that far
Collective memory is formed spontaneously

Like a raging storm
That builds and builds
Collective memory will gather
And have a life of its own
No one can control it

History moves
Collective memory certainly will play a role
Who know what the relationship will be
But there will be consequences
All action has a reaction

Collective memory
Palestinians are developing it
Arabic people are forming it
Asians and Africans too
I figure this is so with other peoples in the world

"Dancing With Two Left Feet"

Dancing with two left feet
You can't help but to step on the partner's foot
It just doesn't jive
There is awkwardness
Flowing from incompleteness

It might be just an expression
But having two left feet
Is not a good thing
Implying that you are a
Bumbling fool

That's how Koreans in the South
Feel as a nation
It might not be necessarily so
But there is the feeling
That the country can be better with a united Korea

Who wants to dance with two left feet?
Surely not Koreans in the South
They want to have fun waltzing through history
With one left foot
And one right foot

They don't want to be stepping on any toes
But wouldn't having good dancing feet avoid that?
A united Korea
Would make a dancer out of the
Bumbling dancer

It's true
It could be all in the mind
But how would one know
If one does not try it?
Koreans want to try unification

"Drenching Rain"

Rain is pouring down outside
Hitting with mercilessness
Roaring in its fury
Like the blows the colonizers once dealt
To the colonized

Sitting here
Looking out the window
Remembering the personal account
Of colonialism
By my grandmother

I can't even begin to fathom
What it must have been like
Being under the dark cloud of colonialism
And like a sick joke
It was everywhere

Sunshine was nowhere to be seen
Because the ominous cloud followed everywhere
Colonialism was all over the country
Koreans were forced to feel subjugated
Like slaves

Some places
There is hardly any rain
This time of the year
Look at Gaza
And Ramallah

There might be days and days of sunshine
But the heavy hand of colonialism is there
And it rains
Pours down
Pain in the hearts of the colonized

Rain is still pouring outside
And it'll continue for hours
From the look of the sky
But I rather have this without colonialism
Than sunshine with colonialist oppression

"Fight for Democracy"

Modern Korean history is
Marked
With fight for democracy
Student demonstrations
House arrests
Exile
All testify to the fight to give
People
Greater rights
Freedom
Now
Korean history is marked by
A step forward
A leader of the people
Who had fought for freedom
Evading threats and death
Is the president
The leader of the nation
Fight for democracy
Seems to have succeeded
But complacency
Has no room
In modern Korean history
Democracy is not represented in one person
It is the collective entity of all individuals
However great or small
So the fight for democracy continues
For standing still
Freedom could easily be curtailed

"Flying Birds"

Birds are flying above
In a flying formation
Like the military planes that I once saw
Forming a fighting pattern

In which direction are they flying?
Birds smoothly gliding through the air
Like F-16's
Breaking through the wind with ease

They look like they are headed north
Surely across the border
That divides the North from the South
Heavily guarded from both sides

Birds are flying there
Thank God they are not war planes
These birds will not drop anything damaging
Except their miniscule bodily waste

The case would be different
Were these battle planes
They would be dropping bombs of mass destruction
Many people would die

Birds are flying fast
And soon they will disappear from my view
They will probably reach the North before sundown
And people there will see

Those in the North might say
Wow, look at these birds
Flying in from the South
Good that they are not war planes

Some unfortunate soul might be hit by bird droppings
But better that than a bomb
Koreans in the South
Don't want fighter planes from the North either

Bombs kill
Many people
Bird droppings
Might ruin a suit, but that's it

Koreans in the South
Might see birds flying in from the North tomorrow
And thank God that
They are not fighting machines

Who wants a war?
Koreans in the South
Koreans in the North
Want to see birds rather than fighter planes ready for action

———— ⬭ ————

"Friendship"

Friendship is a virtue
I figure it's a virtue in every society
In the West friendship has been written about
For over two thousand years
One could say that there is a classic philosophy of friendship

Friendship is certainly a virtue
In the Korean society
But there tends to be an
All or nothing
Understanding of friendship

If you are a friend
Then a Korean would do all that he can for you
The deepness of friendship is represented in the idea
That a friend is one who could die for you
Give his life for yours

One could say that this concept of friendship
Is grounded in Confucianism
I don't know how accurate that is
It is true that Confucianism emphasizes friendship
But I figure it's a combination of several factors

Korean history is long
Over five thousand years long
During that period
Koreans have seen much sadness
As well as joys

In the midst of all the development
Something right did happen
Understanding of friendship that is healthy
For the society
And brings happiness to its people

"Funny"

Funny
It might have seemed
To the colonizers
How the colonized
Cringed in suffering

Funny
It probably was
To those abusing power
To impose themselves
On the oppressed

Funny
It surely must have been
To see the collective pain
Of the people who were
Subjugated

Funny
How funny it is
Laughing and laughing
While the suffering
Look for hope

Funny
It certainly is not for those who are crying out for redemption
Koreans have experienced this
In the heavy hand of colonialism
Just the way Palestinians feel today

Funny
No
It's not funny
For the Palestinians
Who suffer at the hand of the Jews

"Ham Suk-hyun"

Freedom fighter
He certainly was
With his long white beard
Wisdom laden white hair
Face wrinkled from his struggles

He stood with authority
Not because he was holding a gun
Or raising his voice
It was who he was
A man with authority

A leader of the people
He was
Because he cared for them
And wanted to serve their interests
Abnegating his own

He spoke
Like Moses in the Bible
And in fact
He was a man of God
Being a preacher man

Combining the ideals of
Christianity
With good values in
Democracy
He tried to push the nation forward towards good

He wanted to maximize the rights
That Koreans had
He remembered what it was like
Under colonialism
Koreans did not have rights

With the Korean nation
In self-governance
He wanted to make sure
That the country will head
In the right direction

How tragic it would be
If Koreans governed by Koreans
Would fall to the same mistakes
As when Koreans were ruled by the colonizers
So he spoke up

He traveled to cities
He walked the country roads
He spoke before the upper class
He talked with the working class
He envisioned a Korea that benefits all

Ham Suk-hyun
Was his name
Originally he came from a village in northern Korea
Where my grandma had her childhood
What an honor to be related to him

What a vision
He had
I remember hearing him
And even as a child
I was mesmerized

He spoke of goodness
Freedom
Equal rights
Justice
Democracy

Young and old
Men and women
The healthy and the sick
The educated and the uneducated
They were all drawn to his message

They say that they don't make leaders like that anymore
I hope that is not true
For there is no time like now
When Korea needs a dynamic and caring leader
Who cares about the good of the people

"Hand of Help"

Where is the hand of help?
Will no one stretch out his hand to help?
Don't they see the pain?
The suffering in their eyes
The poor people of Palestine are suffering

How could they be so calloused?
As Palestinian children do not have food or drink
As the young of Palestine are besieged
Daily by Israeli soldiers
In an unjust military venture

Europe stands back
And registers an insignificant protest
Which it knows will not change their course
Of oppression
The Palestinians will suffer

It is unjust
That the Palestinians are not given a state
It not only hurts the Palestinians
But it will hurt the Jews
In the long run

But the crazy Jews in Israel
Are pressing on with their crazy fight
Propping up an ideology
Borne from a colonialist project
They are leading the Jewish State down the war path

Give Palestinians their land
To rule on their own
Respect them
And see them not with prejudiced eyes
Jews are no more and no less violent than Arabs

People are people
The Jewish State and the Palestinian State
Could co-exist
Even if the crazy leaders of the State of Israel
Try to convince you otherwise

The colonialists did not think that Koreans were fit to rule
And govern their own people
Perhaps they made an argument from national security
To protect the Japanese people
Japan had to colonize Koreans

How ridiculous it is
To hear it
I am sure many Japanese people now will agree
Since colonialism no longer exists
And Korea and Japan co-exist

But crazy Israeli leaders
Want to solicit a hand of help
For their colonialist venture
And they are looking toward Europe
And the USA

Fie!
Fie!
Don't give your hand of help to the colonizers
With their crazy ideology
That supports racist attack of Palestinians

Lend a helping hand
To the Palestinians
End the colonialism
This is good for Arabs and Jews
Alike

Leaving the situation to the crazy Jewish leaders
There will be no peace for Jews and Arabs
Jewish blood and Arab blood will continue to run
They are both the same color
Red

Lend a helping hand
End the colonialism
Force the crazy Jewish leaders to respect
Arabic people
And dispel their racism against Arabs

The Palestinian State
And the Jewish State
Could coexist
The colonizers and the colonized
Just like Japan and Korea

"House Arrest"

Why is it that
Every time
That an oppressive government
Wants to shut up a voice of the people
They place him in a house arrest?

It happened to the current
President of Korea
When he was a speaker of the people
Standing up boldly for freedom and rights
He did suffer and people saw it

It's like some oppressors feel that they can
Quench the message
But bottling up the speaker
In the confined space
Where he can be observed

Does
Not
Stop
The
Message

President Kim Dae-jung
Is a testimony to this fact
He leads the country now
In the past
This very country tried to shut him up

Some say that it was the
House arrest
Which gave him power
De facto
As people came to see him as a symbol of freedom

In the beginning stages of the country
When Korea was struggling to define himself
It was those like him
Who suffered house arrest
Or other types of censure

Who
Spread
The
Message
Effectively

The house arrest achieved
The opposite of what the governing authorities wanted
Speakers on behalf of the oppressed
Encouraging greater access for all
Shouting liberty throughout the land

They were the voice of the people
The sum of all the individuals
In Korea
There is no power that is greater than that
On this earth

Like a fish in a fishbowl
These freedom fighters were observed
The undemocratic forces in the government
Wanted so much to paint them as inadequate
Even evil

But the power of the message
Could not be contained
Even as their weaknesses were laid bare for all to see
All their secrets revealed in an embarrassing way
The truth could not be contained

House arrest as an official government policy
Had the de facto result
Of advancing democracy in Korea
And the suffering were eager to embrace their personal loss
For the benefit of the people

"I Am Outside"

I am outside
Because I was plucked from my hometown
From the land of my birth
In my ignorance
I was led away

I did not know what was happening to me
When they took me forcefully from my land
The place of my childhood
I knew my dad and my brothers
I could not say that I knew men

As a teenage girl
I had many a dream
I longed for the picture book love
Fairytale life
A happy ending

Who would have thought that my life would end up like this?
Certainly, not I
Not in a million years
I might have dreamed this
In my worst nightmare

I did not even know what love was
When the colonizers took me
As a love toy
For the soldiers
Fighting a colonialist war

I was only in my teens
When I was shipped away from the
Hermit Kingdom
To be in a foreign land
Where no Korean is spoken

I was alone
Utterly lonely
Not knowing what to do
Dropped into a foreign place
Where there was no real love

I was violated
Again and again
By different men
Who all had different reasons for screwing me
Except love

As a teenage woman
The colonizers thought that they had the right
To violate
To take away my right
To ignore my person

Evils of colonialism
I know it personally
It's not an intellectual abstraction
It is not an evil from a book learning point of view
I have lived to see its ugly face

It is always before me
The evil
Violation
Violence
Lack of respect

Colonialism
There is no good in it
It has broken my family
It has taken away my life
It has destroyed my dreams

Colonialism
There is no good in it
But people never learn
The colonized always struggle helplessly
As colonizers justify their colonialism

"Ignorance Is Bliss?"

Is ignorance really bliss?
That's the popular saying to be sure
And some things not known
Make pain non-existent
But that certainly is not the case with colonialism

When Korea was colonized
People suffered
They knew pain
Although they might have been ignorant
Unaware of some things

Koreans did not know
How they were going to free themselves
From the fist of colonialist oppression
How to avoid the blows
That brought them so much pain

Koreans were ignorant of
What it really meant to be the other
They could not verbalize why it was so wrong
For them to be oppressed in such a manner
The immorality of colonialism

Koreans had no clue
How they could bring awareness to the
International community
People who might be able to help
If they were set free from their ignorance

How could Koreans set free
Others
When they could not set themselves
Free?
A helpless position, it is

So is the evil of colonialism
Not only does it subjugate
In real terms
Colonialism
Blocks potential for enlightenment

Ignorance is certainly not bliss
For if the colonized knew how to explain
Enlighten others of the evils of colonialism
Compelling them to do the right thing
Then they would not be colonized

But the colonized are trapped
Inside a box
Created by the colonizers
Those with power
And knowledge

Enlightenment
How important it is for the colonized
To enlighten others
Might mean difference between
Freedom and continued captivity

"Struggle for Democracy"

Struggle for democracy
A road rough and difficult
Why?
Because Korean leaders had seen only the evil hand of the
Colonizing government

Thirty-five years of colonization
That's a whole generation and more
So how could they learn anything
But what they had seen and heard?
The process was difficult from the beginning

Thank God
That there were those who would do their best
To stand for democracy
Making the needed personal sacrifice
Raising their voices in righteous criticism

Thank God
For President Kim Dae-jung
Who in his youth
Sacrificed
For Korea's democracy

Thank God
For Rev. Ham Suk-hyun
Who devoted his whole life
To advance freedom
In the land

What a difficult movement it was
Working toward freedom and justice
For all in the society
The freedom fighters knew from the beginning
It would be difficult

The new Korean government
Emerging from thirty-five years of colonialism
Had to relearn what it meant to represent the people
Not just suck them dry
Leave those who work with nothing for themselves

Thank God
That there were righteous voices
That kept the government honest
At the cost of their personal freedom
They were not silent

All the good that Korea is today
Owes a lot
To the blood sweat
Of those who struggled
With love in their heart

They stood firm
In the midst of suffering
Persecution did not daunt them
Are there leaders like them today?
Korea needs such a conscience of the nation

———— ⚭ ————

"Shining Light"

Brightly
In reminiscent radiance
Of times past
But not lost
Is the power of the
Shining light
That transcends distance
As far as my eyes could see
It is as if my eyes
Emit a sharp arrow
Fired by one skilled as Robin Hood
As I gaze towards the horizon
Over the blue waters
Waves
So calm in its undulating movement
Peaceful
Relaxing
Towards the glaring sunlight
Fired over the waters
As it is setting
Almost as if it wants to show its last
Ounce of strength
Flexing its luminous muscle
How its power confronts my sharp gaze
Two powerful light emissions meet
Over the waters off of the Korean peninsula
Shining light
Reminds me of times past
People who might have gazed toward this very horizon

Life of the country
Luminaries who added to the betterment of society
Of fellow human beings
Might I be added among one of them
And become a
Shining light?

"Seoul Drivers"

Completely crazy
They are
These Seoul drivers
They don't know
What car lanes are

One car is driving right down the drawn lane
Why do they make the lines visible
If these Seoul drivers will not heed them?
It does look pretty on the road
But Seoul drivers will do what they want

These Seoul drivers are masters of their own cars
And the road exists for them
It is not a master
But a servant
The driver is completely in the control seat

Is it machismo?
Why do they drive like madmen?
It could be a way to vent their stress, no?
They talk about road rage in the USA
But it doesn't look like that

It's not that they are frustrated or angry
They just drive that way
It is a part of their road culture
Seoul drivers sure have a lot of
Soul

Well, they have a lot of guts
Hopefully
Which won't be splattered on the street
Because they sure drive like
Crazy maniacs

Three cars driving
Side by side
On a two lane road
You won't catch me doing that
I like my life

These Seoul drivers
Drive like there is no tomorrow
It's like
Carpe Diem
On the road

Fearlessly they switch lanes
They look like they are having the time of their life
But don't put me in one of those cars
I like my life
Nice and slow

Risk adverse
I might miss out on the fun
But I will also escape the accidents
However
They say these Seoul drivers do not get into accidents

Is it possible that they have their cake
And eat it too?
Oh, ho!
They take the risk without thinking
It's a part of the driving culture in Seoul

But give me nice wide roads
And drivers who keep to their lanes
I might not have the excitement
But I will avoid the accidents
Call me risk adverse

These Seoul drivers do
Have a lot of
Umph!
Driving the way they do
Too much kimchee, perhaps?

But you gotta love them
The way they drive like madmen
Dressed in gentlemen clothes
And with their gentle mannerisms
Many bound by family traditions

You might not be on the same road
With these Seoul drivers
But if you need to get anywhere fast
You won't find any more eager driver
Who will get you there in time without an accident

————— ✣ —————

"Revolutionaries"

America was borne out of a revolution
There was a military
Violent
Struggle for
Freedom

Americans did not hesitate
To kill
And overthrow the power
That they deemed oppressive
The English called Americans terrorists

When Koreans were oppressed
Some resisted with all that they had
They were willing to kill
To defend themselves
And free themselves

I bet Japanese colonialists
Back then
Called Korean freedom fighters
Terrorists as well
Just the way the English did Americans

Palestinians are struggling
To free themselves
Their goal is the same
As that which Americans had
During the American Revolutionary War

All that the Palestinians want
Is to govern themselves
Have freedom
Some dignity and respect
That's what Koreans fought for too

Desire for self-governance
And respect
That's what Palestinians are fighting for
It's something that Koreans can understand
Certainly Americans can too

"President Jimmy Carter's Visit"

I remember that day
When President Jimmy Carter
Visited Korea
It was a monumental affair
At the height of pro-Americanism

Koreans gathered together
To observe the procession
As if to say
Thank you for fighting for us
During the Korean War

Christians gathered
Some thirty per cent of Korea is Christian
If not more
To see the Baptist President
Who teaches Sunday School to kids

President Jimmy Carter had a good reputation in Korea
People saw him as a Southern gentleman
Koreans like the South
Stories of cowboys
Southerners reputed to be kind and friendly

It was almost like a national holiday
Seeing the American President
Passing through the crowded Korean streets
Receiving more honor than the
Korean President in office

Koreans waved Korean flags
And American flags
Some held both flags together
And waved them high in the air
As if the two countries were one

Some shouted that America was number one
Other Koreans sang the Korean national anthem
American national anthem could be heard as well
Oh, how those Koreans loved Jimmy Carter
And the country that he represented

———— ❦ ————

"Pepper Juice"

No
It's not a breakfast item
That Koreans consume
But it is a juice of sort
Pepper juice

What is it?
You might ask
It is made of grounded pepper
Hot and spicy
As they get

Mixed with water
So it would flow
Where?
You might ask
That has a logical answer

To flow down
The nose of a Korean
Hung upside down
To torture him
It probably went straight to the brain

One of the nifty methods
Of inflicted suffering
During the colonialist days
Against those who resist
It's no joke

Eyes would water at first
Perhaps there would be a sneeze or two
But these relatively mild bodily reaction
Induced artificially
Would quickly degenerate

Some would soon pass out
Wouldn't you?
I bet I would
That pepper juice must have been
Nasty!

Not a way to go
I would say
But those Koreans
Under colonialist persecution
Did not have a choice

"Northern Brothers"

Koreans in the South
Look towards the North
They don't feel disdain
Or hatred
But sorrow at the separation

Those Koreans in the North
Are Koreans
Some of them are family members
Separated only by an artificial boundary
Formed by political interest of others

Koreans in the South
Have experienced the joys and sorrows of
Capitalism
Economic miracle and the financial crisis

Those Koreans in the North
Have only seen poverty
Communism has dealt a heavy blow
The pain is shared by Koreans down under

Koreans in the South
Do not want to see massive deaths of
Koreans in the North
Due to famine or human induced crisis

Those Koreans in the North
Might add economic burden
In the event of unification
But that's okay

Koreans in the South
Will bear the burden willingly
Because Koreans belong together
The land can be united

Those Koreans in the North
Are brothers
Northern Brothers
If you will

Koreans in the South
Desire a peaceful unification
Without war
Without deaths

Those Koreans in the North
Probably want the same
So thinks
Southern brothers

Koreans in the South
Think
Pray
Hope

"*Imposition*"

Colonialism is
Imposition
Colonialists impose themselves
On the colonized
With a sense of ownership

The colonialists feel that they
Have the right to define
The colonized
Much more so than
The colonized themselves

Imposition
In every aspect of life
Even setting the official language
Of commerce and daily dealing
The colonized do not really have a choice

Helpless because of the situation
In which the colonialists
Have imposed themselves
Unwelcome
With force and aggression

Colonialist power
Imposing their will
Upon the colonized
Imposition of law
Wrongly made and applied

Legal
Sure it is
It is legal for the colonialists
To oppress
They made those laws

Imposition
Depriving of self
Respect
Freedom
That's what colonialists do

The oppressed
Should not take this
Imposition
Koreans opposed colonialism
Even when it looked futile

Thus
The Palestinians oppose
With stones picked up from the streets
Outdated weapons
Which really have no chance of victory

Colonialists
Continue to impose
The colonized resist
With all that they have
Even if that's not quite enough

———— ❧ ————

"Korean High Schools"

It has been reputed that
Korean high schools
Are a hell on earth
Students study and study
From morning to night

Some working from before sunrise
And not getting back home until sunset
Some blame Confucianism and the value placed on education
For causing the high school students to labor and toil
Others say that hope for success is the driving factor

Even in TV series
One sees a critical view on the excess work required in
Korean high schools
Students do their homework
And even have extra lessons for college entrance exams

Some say that
Which university one gets into determines one's life
Many Koreans agree
So Korean high schools represent the critical stage
And how they toil!

It seems almost cruel
To make all those high school students compete
Not really against each other
Capitalist model of competition has not yet taken hold
They compete against the system

To score the best test score
Required to get into the college of their choice
Some say that a college in Seoul is enough
It doesn't even have to be the top three
All in the capital city

Korean high schools
Churn out nerds
Because it's the test score that determines
Which college one gets into
Not extracurricular activities

Some say that it's a fair system
Your test scores get you in
It's an objective standard
Perhaps there is truth to this
Everyone is measured by one standard

However
The problem is that
Test scores do not determine the future success of the student
In real life situations
Linked to the success of corporations and even the nation

Is it possible that important persons
Slip through the cracks
Because they do not have the best scores
And therefore are denied access to certain institutions
Where they might be able to contribute in a big way?

Who knows?
One thing is for sure
Korea is a country that loves nerds
Korean high schools give credit to the nerd factor
So Korea will churn out brainiacs and bookworms

To lead the country
And hope that the brain standard
Is the most important
Even if a student can't get one basket inside the basketball net
Hopefully he will help net a successful future for Korea

It all begins in the Korean high school
Where people's fortunes are promised
Future is determined
Path is set
For better or for worse

———— ⚭ ————

"Laundry"

There is laundry hanging to dry
In the courtyard
It's funny
Looking back
How the house was structured

There was the front gate
In the house
Which was removed from the rooms
The bedrooms were on the other side
Opposite the front yard

The toilet was reached by exiting the rooms
Walking across the open courtyard
Whether in the winter with snow blizzard
Or in the summer with scorching heat
One had to tough it out

Kitchen was located
At a perpendicular angle
To the bedrooms
And the attached living room
One had to cross the open courtyard to get to them

The open courtyard
Served many purposes
It was a place where laundry was hung
To dry
As sun beat down from the sky

It was a place where children could play
If one had a dog
He had a doghouse
In the open courtyard
It's also the place where all the kimchee jars were kept

Now
The laundry hung there
In the openness
Of the court
As the wet clothes dried

I could see with my mind's eye
In the ever present
The past
The house of my childhood
The laundry hanging in the open courtyard

"Meeting"

Some might consider this a little odd
Particularly in the West
How Korean high school students
Participate in
Meeting

A group of girls
Agree to meet
An equal number of guys
In a coffee house
Where the price is exorbitant

Classic music
Or a soft pop music
Would play in the background
As the ingathered
Chat above their awkwardness

Coming from an all boys' school
For many this could be a social highlight
Girls would be coming from an all girls' school
And they would fancy the social outing
There would be conversations for days afterwards about it

At least a decade or so ago
It used to be this way
Who knows if this still goes on?
I figure the high school students of today would know
Whether meetings take place

"My Life Belongs To Me"

My life belongs to me
Why can't you see that?
I know
Korea is currently colonized
Does it give you authority over me?

Why do you feel that you can control
What language I use
What I think
My actions
My life?

Do you feel that you have the right
To observe my every behavior
Record everything that I say
Read my mail
Deprive me of my personal space?

Yes
You are colonizing
Korea
Perhaps you feel that you own me
And all other Koreans?

We are objects to you?
All of Koreans whom you oppress
And colonize
Presently
We are violated by the hand of colonialism

Oh
You colonizers
Koreans are not objects
We have life
We are living beings
Thinking beings

Do you feel that you own us?
You have the right to treat us any way you want?
We don't even know you
You don't know us
Why do you take liberties with us?

Colonialism is your excuse?
Your reason?
Your rationale?
You think that because of colonialism
We Koreans have no right?

You want us to suffer in silence?
You don't want us to think for ourselves?
You want us to do what you want?
You don't want us to have free will?
You want us to agree to your colonialist venture?

My life belongs to me
Yeah
You hear me
It belongs to me
You colonizers

You are colonizing the Korean people
But I will not remain silent
Kill me if you have to
I will register my protest
Colonialism does not give you the right

Colonialism convicts you
You are found guilty by your own hand
Your security measures are the evidence against you
All see it
And they understand

My life belongs to me
Despite your efforts to control my life
Make me cowtow to your strong army
Your hateful use of your laws
My life belongs to me

"Korean Uncle Toms"

Yes, it is shameful
What is?
The fact that some Koreans
Participated
In colonialism

Yes, there were Korean Uncle Toms
Those who were Koreans
Who abetted the colonizers
Oppressing Koreans
At a profit

Some might have reasoned
From a selfish perspective
It is better to save oneself
Since the mass could not be saved
I am insignificant anyway

Others might not have felt too much moral compunction
They could have had cold hearts
Closing their eyes to the suffering of fellow Koreans
And to the oppressing power of the colonizers
It must not have been easy to do, right?

How could they have done this?
Without these participating Korean Uncle Toms
Colonialism probably would not have been so smooth
They provided vital information needed for enslavement
Of Koreans to the colonizers

Why is it that there are such as these?
Why do some participate in doing evil?
It seems like in every case of enslavement
Colonialism
You will see them

It's probably the case with the Palestinians
There must be some Arab Uncle Toms
Who facilitate the oppression of the Arabic people
At the hand of the State of Israel
Do they not feel anything in their heart?

"Needed"

Needed
A brave soul
Who cares about the future
Thinking not only of self but others
Willing to toil to improve the country

Needed
A conscientious soul
Who understands the historical reality
And the ethical ramifications of her place in history
The power of the present to move current events

Needed
A daring soul
Who is willing to jump at the chance
To make the society a better place
Not worrying about the risks

Needed
A thinking soul
Who ponders the good that could come about
When people unite to do good
And how this unification should be encouraged

Needed
A strong soul
Who is willing to take on the burdens of others
And the society badly in need of leadership
Seeing leading as serving with boldness

Needed
A careful soul
Who plans out the details
Needed to bring about realistic changes for the better
Idealism coupled with strategy

Needed
Souls like these
If Korea is to see a bright future
There has to be positive luminaries
Thinking combined with action

"North Koreans Are People Too"

North Koreans are people too
Sure thing
You don't think they are some kind of
Monsters
Do you?

Some Americans were shocked to see East Germans
After the Berlin Wall fell
They thought they would encounter some
Extra Terrestrial beings
There were capitalist propaganda against East Germans

There are Germans
From East Germany
Everywhere
They work in the previous West Germany
Live abroad

Even in America
You will find former
East Germans
Living and working
Contributing to economy like good capitalists

In the past
Perhaps
Some Americans thought of East Germans
As a kind of
Monsters

What has changed?
The communist government fell
People in the East united with the people in the
West
Germany became one

So why not Korea?
If there is unification
North Koreans might be found in Wall Street
Contributing to America's economic well-being
It would not seem strange at all

It's all in the perception
North Korea
Could look like an evil nation
And its people too
If some people want to look through those lenses

Change your glasses
And see
North Koreans
East Germans
They are all people, just like you and me

"Teachers"

Teachers are respected in the Korean society
As authority figures
An element of stability in society
Who cement the harmony of the Korean society

Vestige of Confucianism?
Perhaps
Learning is a virtue in Confucianism
And teachers who communicate knowledge are a part of that virtue

Traditionalism as the catalyst behind the respect?
Maybe
Korean society is still quite traditional
Emphasizing respect of elders and leaders

Common sense as a factor?
It could be
Because teachers teach the future leaders of Korea
Anyone who cares about Korea's future would give them due respect

It is a part of the culture
That is true
It is normative to respect the teacher
Not respecting teachers is seen as abnormal

It is funny how norms are defined in societies
This respect for teachers might be seen as irrational
In non-Korean societies
But then, they will not experience the tranquility that comes with
such a respect

Teachers
And respecting them
Hold a society together
In unquantifiable ways

Who can measure
The cause and the effect?
Respect of teachers
Making a society a healthier one

But I guess
People might realize
The cost
That not respecting teachers has on a society

For a society that does not respect teachers
Will experience societal dysfunction
A kind of sickness that will become evident in societal tragedy
Perhaps Koreans are right to see not respecting teachers as abnormal?

Some Koreans say
That a society's health could be measured
By the respect it shows to teachers
I wonder if crime rate is related to it

———— ⸙ ————

"Superman"

It's a bird
It's a plane
No
It's superman

Wow
The first movie
Superman
In a big movie theatre

People packed in
Like sardines
With screen bigger than
Any I have seen

All Koreans
Eager to see the movie
About a superhuman being
Who helps people

Superman on the screen
Looked nothing like
Any Korean
That I knew

But yet
Superman
Represented a hero
For the Korean people

Children admired the flying movie star
Adults even had a warm place in their heart
For this imaginary figure
Always there to do good

A symbol
He was
Superman
Who could circle the earth in a fraction of a second

Superman
Captured the imagination of a people
Totally different in culture
From that represented in the movie

Nonetheless
Superman as a hero
Hero for the Koreans
Who elevated him as their own hero symbol

"Take Me Back To My Childhood"

It can't be done
I know
But I want to say it anyway
Take me back to my childhood
Before colonialism has ruined me

As a voice
Small voice
Of one who remembers the time before
My teenage girl years
When I was oblivious

How nice it was
With no care in the world
I cannot help but shed tears
With a loud wail in my heart
I want to go back

Before colonialists took me
Along with other teenage girls
Of the Hermit Kingdom
To be used and abused
We were all optimistic before then

Give me back my optimism
Happiness
My past
That the colonialists have taken away
I want my childhood back

Before I was force-fed
The fruit of the knowledge of good and evil
Rather the fruit was all evil
As I was held down
They ignored my cries and protests

I want my childhood back
When as a little girl
I wandered free
Played house
With other girls with lots of dreams

Before the colonizers took them all away
They forced me to do what I did not want to do
In the name of law they did this
Of course
The colonizers have the law on their side

Take me back to my childhood
Give me the chance to make my own mistakes
I don't want to be a puppet
We were all puppets of colonialism
All the young women of Korea used as Japanese Army Toys

"Tears in Her Eyes"

Grandma
Can you tell me a little bit about
Japanese colonialism?
What happened?
Do you remember?

Yes
Grandson
I remember well
Korean people were forced
Into many things that they did not want to do

Like what
Grandma?
Can you give details?
Did they force Koreans
With guns?

Yes
Grandson
The Japanese colonizers
Used guns
And force

Grandma
Why did they do it?
Why did the Koreans
Obey the Japanese?
I would have fought them

Yes
Grandson
I know
That's what many people said before....
You be strong

Grandma
I am embarrassed
That Koreans
Just obeyed
And allowed themselves to be colonized

Yes
Grandson
I understand
But don't be ashamed of Koreans
They did not have the weapons that the colonizers had

Grandma
Why did they not have weapons?
They should have been prepared
Why did they allow the colonizers to have
All the weapons?

Yes
Grandson
You have that mentality
To defend the Koreans and Korea
With kids like you, Korea will be strong

Grandma
Why are there tears in your eyes?
Are you sad?
Did horrible things happen then?
Did colonizers hurt you?

Yes
Grandson
It was a very sad period in Korean history
The colonizers did not hesitate to hurt Koreans
All Korean families were adversely affected

"Why Unify?"

What's the deal with unification anyway?
Why do all these Koreans want unification?
Two is better than one, isn't it?
Why unify?

South Korea
North Korea
One people divided into two
Families separated by a political partition

Did the Korean people create this partition?
No
Then who did?
The superpowers

Two superpowers
Holding onto opposite political ideologies
Carved up a land belonging to one people
Families were divided

A dagger was driven into the heart of a people
People who have not experienced such a forced separation
Even when they had suffered
They did so together in unity

But the Korean people were split into two
To cater to the whims of the two superpowers
It was all official
Legal under international law of the time

With a few signatures
Families were divided
Never to be able to see the others again
North and South

The line of demarcation
Stands out ostensibly in the map of Korea
It's like two incomplete puzzle pieces
With same color and texture

Both places
Korean is spoken
There would be no problem with communication
Were the North and the South to unite

Families would be united
There are those who have not seen their loved ones
For years, years, and years
Such a long time

No wonder
Koreans sing of unification
Both in the North and the South
Unification drives the Korean soul

Ideology goes only so far
Look at Germany
When communism fell in the East
Germans were united without real ideology problems

Governments might prop up political ideology
For it keeps those government officials in power
But people are people
Families want to be united

Daily people live
Eat
Sleep
Go to work

This happens regardless of the political leaning
Even in the USA
You might have division in political thinking
Within the same family

But unlike Americans
Koreans see a divided land
Where even families cannot see each other
If they are on the other side

Why unify?
The answer is simple really
Because families want to be together
Koreans want to be one people again

"The French Embassy"

The French Embassy
Was just around the corner
From where I lived in Seoul
I remember running down the street
Making a turn
And beholding the flag
That represents
Democratic struggle
French was surely spoken inside
Although I have never heard French outside
I was in school
When the Embassy people hung out
Outside
Perhaps
It was my first introduction to
Foreign essence
Who would have thought that
It would be only the beginning
Of many non-Koreans that
I would encounter in the course of my
Life-time
I wonder if the French Embassy
Is still there
If so
Surely
French is spoken inside
And if I hang out
Outside
Long enough
I am sure I will catch some French people
Outside
Speaking French

"The West"

Isn't it the West
That sold Korea to Japan?
In effect
They blessed the colonialism
Accepted the colonialist leaders with respect

So it is with the leaders of the State of Israel
Israeli Prime Minister visits Germany
And is treated like a king
Don't Germans know that he is a colonizer?
What's the difference with the past?

People do not learn from history
That is the problem
Players change
Victims change
But colonialist oppression goes on

And the West
Keeps its mouth shut
As it welcomes colonizers
Give them a voice in the media
Letting them paint the colonized in a bad light

Koreans remember how the West
Sold it out
Even as we bite our tongue
And forgive the West
For its complicity in the evil colonialist venture

Past is past after all
But now
Why is the West
Repeating the colonialist evil of the past
Why are they not raising its protest?

The West
What will it do?
In the Palestinian case
Will they allow the injustice to happen?
How could they!

"*Understanding Palestinians*"

All Koreans understand the suffering of
The Palestinians
The oppressed
The colonizers
So do all those who had been colonized before

It is true that Koreans do not have any ties to Palestinians
Neither do Indians
Africans
Language is different
Culture too

But they are all bound
In the suffering of the oppressed
Colonialism has left an imprint
On Korean history
Indian history

African history
The colonized remember
As they think back
They see the Palestinians suffering now
It is so fresh in the collective memory

Isn't it funny how the past
Colonizers
Are all flocking to the aid
Of the current colonizer?
Actually, it's sad

Did not the West learn
How horrible colonialism is?
Why do they aid and abet?
The colonized cannot understand
As the Palestinian people suffer

Give freedom
To the colonized
It is the right thing to do
Give them what is rightfully theirs
The land belongs to them

No amount of intellectual gymnastics
Can justify the unrighteous suffering
The colonized people of the world are united
In sympathy
In empathy

They remember
Koreans
Indians
Africans
The evil of colonialism

Although they may not know Arabic
Despite the fact that there might be different practices
Cultural norms
They understand the Palestinians
And why they fight and resist

"Why Did You Do This?"

I want to ask my colonizers
Why did you do this?
I want to look straight into their eyes
And confront my persecutors
Now I finally have the courage

When as a teenage girl
The colonizers took me away
From my village in Korea
To be used as a toy for the
Japanese army

I could not open my eyes
It's true that I was shy
But I should have spoken up
Even then
To die would have been better

But I was silent
I was afraid
I was weak
I was ignorant
I did not know what to do

Then
I just closed my eyes
Pressed my upper lip against my lower lip
And tried to bear
The pain

As the dirty smell of the Japanese soldiers
Pressed down on my body
Filled my nose
I could not scream
No!

All I could do is close my eyes
And suffer
And suffer
And suffer
And suffer

Korea was helpless
It could not protect me
A Korean
Because Japan
Had colonized and abused its power

I am no politician
Have no interest in politics
Even now
But politics affected me
In a big way

I was violated
As a teenager
For many years
By the official policy of the Japanese government
I even forgot how to hate as I suffered

My youth
My first love
My first kiss
My first love making
My first boyfriend

They were all taken away by colonialism
Why did they think that they had the right?
How could they violate me the way that they did?
Now, my past is gone
And my future looks bleak

I will go on
Because I have to
I will find the strength
But colonialism has marred forever
This person

It seems like yesterday
That I was a bright eyed
Teenage girl
Looking forward to my first kiss
From the one that I loved

All I got was a bunch of dirty
Smelly
Japanese soldiers
Who did not bother to say a word
Before they violated me over and over again

I want to confront everyone who violated me
Face to face
Why did you do what you did?
Don't I look like a human being to you?
Why do you think that colonialism gives you the right?

H.C. Kim

"Won't Take It Lying Down"

We won't take it lying down
As the colonialists oppress us
Deprive us of our rights
Who do they think that they are?
They could threaten us with death?

There is a value to fight for
To die for
Fighting colonialism is worth it
Americans did it
And Americans founded their nation on this struggle

Koreans fought
With sticks and voices
In order to have self rule
Freedom
Human dignity

We won't take it lying down
We will learn from the Americans
We will learn from the Koreans
To fight
Struggle for freedom

We are Palestinians
And our struggle is a fight against colonialist power
Power certainly against the justice of Heaven
We have honor on our side
To fight for our basic human rights

Just like Americans killed to defend themselves
Koreans struggled with all they had
Against colonialism
We Palestinians will fight
We will not take it lying down

You Americans understand don't you?
After all you struggled the same way
Your country was founded in such a manner
And you Koreans fought for freedom
Our Palestinian struggle is no different

———— ⌘ ————

"Yellow Star"

Put the yellow star on my shirt mom
I want to feel special
I want to feel like I have the power
I want people to be reminded
Who I am

So I can do whatever I want
I want to shut everyone up
With my yellow star
Prominently displayed for all to see
I don't want anyone to stop me

Put the yellow star prominently on my shirt
Yellow attracts attention
Causes people to remember
It is almost like history
In its force

That will shut them up
And allow me to do what I want to do
Make people remember
I want no obstruction
To my venture

It could be a five pointed star
6 pointed star
Ten pointed
It doesn't matter to me
Just as long as it will give me license

Mom
Do you think that the yellow star
Will give a small Korean boy power?
No son the yellow star does not give you the power that you seek
Koreans do not abuse the yellow star for personal gain